Yah's Daughter

Awakening Lessons from the Father

Ebony N. Stubbs

Copyright © 2022 Ebony N. Stubbs | Yah's Daughter

All rights reserved. No part of this publication may be reproduced, distributed, or transmitted in any form or by any means, including photocopying, recording, or other electronic or mechanical methods, without the prior written permission of the publisher, except in the case of brief quotations embodied in critical reviews and certain other noncommercial uses permitted by copyright law. For permission requests, write to the publisher, addressed "Attention: Permissions Coordinator," at the email address below.

Prepared by: Ebony Nicole Smith Consulting | ebonynicolesmith.com

Editor: A.B. Brumfield | Omni3Publishing | omni3publishing.com

Front cover image by Chris Johnson | Photography by Chris Johnson

Book cover design by HMDGFX Publishing

ISBN: 979-8-218-03857-1 (Paperback)

Printed by CreateSpace in the United States of America.

Permission: Ebony N. Stubbs – yahdaughter3@gmail.com

First printing edition 2022.

Dedication

The dedication of this book is split in six ways.

My Brothers:

Bernard

Ivorick

Derrick

My Sons:

Dakari

Ricky

Marshawn

From boys to men, you will always be connected to my heart.

Acknowledgments

First and foremost, praises and thanks go to our Heavenly Father, Yah, for the many doors He opened and the blessings He handed out along my journey. Thank you, Father Yah, for correcting my vision and my hearing so that my mission was effective unto you.

To my husband, Ricky Stubbs Sr., I am ever so grateful to you. You made sure that I had many quiet nights to write and get this book done. Your love, support, and encouragement are a constant testament to your faithfulness to the Most High and to me as your wife. You are appreciated, valued, and loved in return.

To my three sons, Dakari Buchanan, Ricky Stubbs Jr, and Marshawn Stubbs, thank you for giving me a reason to push my way through life and do all that I do. I also want to thank you guys for being so attentive when I shared pieces of my life with you as I wrote the book. You guys asked questions and showed me that you cared. You will forever be my three heartbeats.

To my mother and stepfather, Leretta and Jesse Williams, thank you for being anchors through the writing process and for being the mental support that held me up and cheered me on along the way. Those are some of the things that helped me get through. Thank you for your endless love as parents.

To my best friend, Ella Whitcomb, my listening ear through the book rant, the best memory that will always be with me was the day both of our families were together hanging out, but you and I slid away. You were busy on your laptop working on your online schoolwork and me on my laptop working on my book writing. We pushed one another to get our work done. Now, that's what friends are for.

To my spiritual brother, Mark Simmons, who served as a nonpaid editor and voice of reason, you have always been an encourager with your very own sense of humor that is always right on time.

To Uncle Jerry, who also served as a nonpaid editor, you helped me to see what certain readers may see. Your input was resourceful. Karen Bunton, thank you for being a phone call away and for praying for my strength.

To Ashley Johnson, sister-friend, I need you to know that the day I was physically tense from the emotions of writing this book, you stood beside me at work and gave to me the same words of encouragement that I'd given you one day. That was a power move, and you didn't even know it. For that, you have my gratitude.

To my two good friends, Cassie and Lekeisha who are a Boulder Coffee meeting away. Thank you, ladies, for the words of encouragement when the load got a little heavy.

To the village that it took to raise me, you will never be forgotten as long as my memory serves me right.

To you, the reader, I want to say thank you for your time and for reading this divine piece of work.

Notes to My Parents

Dear Mom,

    I write this letter from a healed heart. I'm so grateful that what I endured and witnessed throughout my childhood didn't minimize who I am today. It was heartbreaking for me to see the pressures of life blind your eyes for so long. There was a wall that you created to tune out reality, but that never stopped me from seeing and knowing that deep down inside, you were a loving and caring woman. You uniquely gave the best love you knew to all four of your children. I've had the chance to witness your transformation from a powerless addiction to your powerful affection. I thank Father Yah for bringing you through the darkness and into His marvelous light.

Love always,

Your forgiving daughter.

Dear Dad,

    I write this letter from an empty place in my heart. I have the one and only letter that I have ever received from you, which I have managed to hold tight to ever since I received it in the mail back in March of 1996. The ending of the letter read:

```
Benjamin Andrews
124 W 120 St
New York, N.Y. 10027


                                                          March 7|1996


  Dear Ebony,

         As I'm sure this letter will come as a very un-exspected surprise, a
  very long and over due, one. Anyway you never sent me the long ago pictures you
  said you were,  I gess I'm the only responsible one between you and I, (Smile).
  Each time I begain this letter it was at night , and I never got it finished,so
  this time I started in the daytime. You know when a person gets tired they star
  -t getting mistakes, and then the letter has alot of mistakes. You really made
  me feel very good when I last spoke to you on the phone.It's funny because Im
  trying to get a new phone and at the same time, I want to take the block off
  the one I have, and each time I say it I never get to do it the next day. When
  a person type's a letter it's not the same as when you hand write it, because
  it seems the space is much smaller, so you try to have to think of much more to
  talk about. Im sending you some pictures of your family, Brothers, Sisters, and
  Cousins; Im going to write on the back of the pictures to let you know whom  is
  who. Also Im going to send you your Brothers phone number (LUMP-Benjamin Andrew
  -s number, I'll let him know you'll be calling him from time to time collect,
  it's allright. Today is March 8|1996, and it's snowing very hard more than like
  ly your in school right now and  there's not much to really do all day, but
  watch T.V.. I really wish you lived closer to me than you do, it would make a
  big diffrence. I'm planning to spend part of the summer with you, I
```

"I really wished you lived closer to me than you do, it would make a big difference. I'm planning to spend part of the summer with you. Love, Dad."

Who would have ever thought that the summer I waited for was going to be the summer I went to your funeral? I'm pretty sure if you were still here you would have held me tight as can be. I want you to know that life was a bit dysfunctional for me. I went down the road of looking for love in all the wrong places, just wanting someone to love me for me. Instead, I received constant hurt. But I'm better now, I know who I am, and I realize that although I lacked your physical touch, the Heavenly Father, Yah, has connected me with His love and truth.

Sincerely always,

Your loving daughter.

Revelation

There was this phrase by Malcolm X that I heard once while growing up in the Black community. It said, "If you want to hide something from black people, put it in a book." After not picking up a book for the thirty-seven years of my life, after not reading on my own personal time, and after not understanding the Bible in its totality, I'm in agreement with the phrase above. Man! I should have listened to Levar Burton and his Reading Rainbow theme song that said, "Take a look, it's in a book, a Reading Rainbow!"

I was never big on reading. To be honest, I never found anything to read that was of great interest besides the Bible. I guess you can say things were hidden very well from me. The amazing part is that God never keeps things from us, we just have to apply ourselves. He showed me His hand and I have held on to it ever since. There is not a doubt in my mind that the three things I am about to elaborate on were heavenly orchestrated, causing a paradigm shift in my life.

In 2019, there were three specific moments that caused my brain and eyesight to connect to a full understanding and that led me to my spiritual identity and divine purpose. Those things were a training, a scripture, and a documentary.

First, I entered a drawing and was picked for a twenty-week *Powerful Parental* course by the name of *PLTI-Parent Leadership Training Institute*. And in that course, I heard someone mention a documentary that grabbed my attention. That documentary led me to read a specific scripture in the Bible. That scripture would later assist in my spiritual awakening.

The scripture was *Genesis 15:13-14 (SHV): And he said unto Abram, know of a surety that thy seed shall be a stranger in a land that is not theirs, and shall serve them; and they shall afflict them four hundred years; And also that nation, whom they shall serve, will I judge: and afterward shall they come out with great substance.*

And lastly, the name of the documentary was "The 1619 Project". It entailed tons of knowledge that everyone, but specifically black people, should know.

Here's how it all works together for my good and understanding.

If you were to take the year that I started the class, 2019, and subtract it from the documentary title number, 1619, it will give you the number in the scripture, 400. That math problem had me in awe and it was the pivotal point in my search for more information in the bible and on the internet. I wanted to know who was being afflicted and why, who was *the seed* that the scripture was referring to, and what was the significance of the time frame of the revelation.

It didn't take long for the meaning of the scriptures to lead me to the divine revelation that the scripture was meant for me. It said that you will be in bondage for 400 years. Well, in 2019 I began my journey of being set free from the bondage of not understanding the Word of Yah. My comprehension of the Bible had opened enormously. As I started to walk in freedom, I began to understand who I am and how I can read the Word of Yah and feel the connection that comes with identifying with scriptures.

Between having all the books and all the technology full of information in front of me, I was starting to feel empowered and hungry for more daily. I was drawn to books that were full of black history and slavery information and I started to see that all things were easily connected to the Word of Yah.

That's when I heard the voice of Yah clearly say, "It's time to write your book."

As you journey through the pages herein, I pray that you will look over what you read as a road map of my life and realize that every detour I encountered was designed with great purpose. For me, there was no getting to my destiny without understanding my detours.

The children of Israel, while on a journey that should have lasted only eleven days, were taken on a forty year detour where they endured plagues, scars, and wounds. Although they made it to their destiny, there was a remnant of trauma left behind followed by some scattering.

This book is written for everyone who belongs to the Most-High Yah but appears to have been lost in a deceptive world ruled by darkness. I have been positioned as a light source, one of Yah's ambassadors, to point you back in the direction of the narrow road that leads to your Creator. I will assist you in understanding your worth, value, and identity in Him as we look at the goodness of our grace, through His Son, Yahshua (Jesus).

Genesis

"That you are a slave, Neo. Like everyone else, you were born into bondage. Into a prison that you cannot taste or see or touch. A prison for your mind."

Morpheus, from The Matrix

Have you ever stopped to think about the framework of your life, what makes you, you? The things you have encountered in life and why? Can you remember growing up in your neighborhood, where you made the best out of what you had, the best way you knew how? Times where food stamps were the only source of income to get food, where taking bottles back to the corner store to get change for your pocket and taking care of your siblings was a must? How about going for hours without knowing where your mother was? Following all that, you grew into adulthood only to wonder if you would repeat the same cycles of life that your parents did and that their parents did. Well, if you didn't, I did.

Let's just say that crack cocaine was intentionally distributed in one of the major cities of the United States, right in the heart of the socially eroded communities of New York City. This drug caused 80% of the African American population to become addicted and strung out. Cocaine has been known to be so powerful that it can cause destructive effects on various parts of the body including your brain, heart, cardiovascular system, and digestive system.

Now, let's add a pregnant woman to this scenario, one who becomes addicted to this toxic drug. And let's say that, once born, her child would face a variety of life-threatening risks and develop lifelong concerns. Now, what If I told you that the addicted mother was my mother? What if I told you that the child in the womb was me? Would you believe me? I hope you would because it is me. Most people would never know that about me except for the fact that I'm now on this spiritual journey that includes sharing some of my life story.

I was born in the heart of New York City which is called Harlem, at a place called Mt. Sinai Hospital, but I was raised in Rochester NY. I would love to give you more background about my early childhood, but that part of my life is somewhat of a mystery to me. From birth to age five seems to have a lot of loopholes. It's still unclear to me what made my mom leave the big city and come to Rochester, what made her try her first drug, and what made her leave my older brother behind to be raised by other family members. There are so many unanswered questions and so many mixed emotions.

The more I write and allow you into my life, the harder this becomes for me. It makes me think of a process called excavation, a process where things are exposed through constant digging so that whatever knowledge of the past obtained is obtained by that digging. This work is done carefully and precisely and the more I think about it and feel the emotions, the more I understand my healing is necessary and intentionally done by my Heavenly Father, Yah.

As I stated before, there is a lot that I don't know and may never know, but I'm ok with that. What I do have, however, is the memory that for the majority of my early childhood, I tended to my younger brother's needs while my mother was out chasing her drug addiction and hanging with her friends. I was about ten years old around that time, taking care of my two younger brothers who were about three and six years old. I remember having to change one of their diapers and making sure they were both fed. I couldn't ask this question then, but as I think about it now, I wonder who was there to give me the true love and affection that I needed as a little girl?

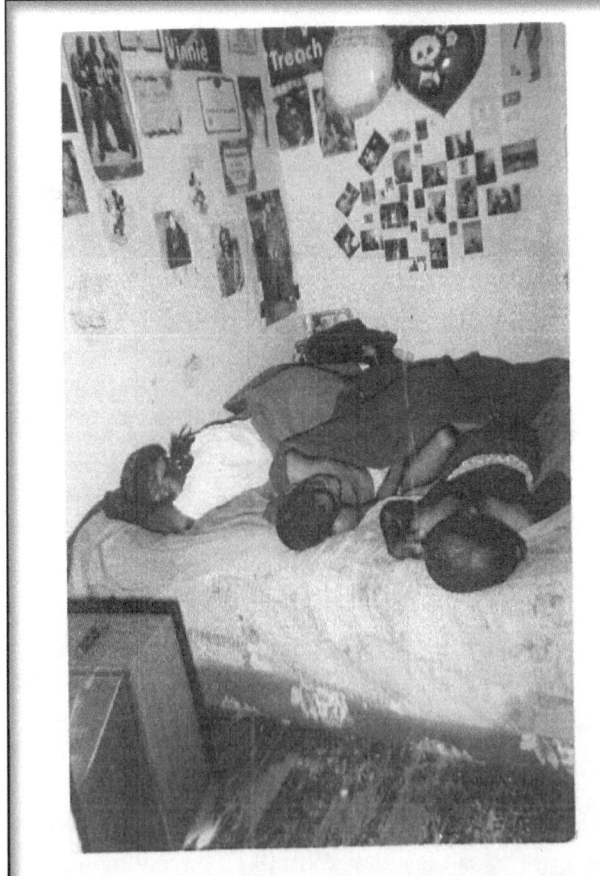

For me, this photo shows proof of why the love I have for my younger brothers is so strong.

An African proverb says, "It takes a village to raise a child."

The walk home from school #9 was slow and steady because I knew exactly what was going to happen once I got home. Mom was going to leave me home with my brothers again. I also knew that upon my arrival, there would be a house full of people. In fact, the majority of the time company was guaranteed to be at the house. In the black community, it was common to address every adult in the house when entering. In our house, I'd better make sure to say hi to mom's friends, also known as uncles and aunts. We were taught to address her friends as that whenever they were around.

I can remember the aroma that filled the room. At that time, I didn't understand what it was, but after getting older, I was able to put a name to it. It was the smell of smoke from their crack pipe and it was obviously from them having their little party prior to me arriving home. While entering the kitchen, I noticed that the smell still lingered in the room. Along with the big eyes, the one hand behind the back, and the look as if they'd lost something, their body gestures always gave away the fact that they were high. After a while, I became accustomed to it all, the smell became normal to me and so did the looks.

It was a guarantee that after arriving home, Mom was soon to go right out the door. I wouldn't see her until nightfall. During Summer, it was a little different as I may have seen her throughout the day while she was coming and going. She would come home to freshen up and change her clothes, then she would go right back outdoors with her friends. If there was one thing for sure about my mother, it was that she took good care of her hygiene and appearance, this woman was color coordinated to the tee. Most times when Mom wasn't home, I knew where she was, but there were many times I didn't have a clue. It was for that reason I would be so happy that she made it home safely every night.

Those countless hours Mom would be gone didn't worry us too badly because we had a village available and waiting with open arms to care for us in our mother's absence. Today, I get overjoyed when I think about the many times Momma Melody kept her eyes on us as we played outside, making sure we were safe when our own momma was nowhere in sight. Momma Melody was so soft-spoken and attentive to me, but maybe that was because she had all boys, and I was the only girl around.

It wasn't just Momma Melody, though, we also had Momma Alice who was liable to cut us down with her words, so we had no choice but to be on our best behavior when she was around. However, she genuinely welcomed us with open arms whenever we needed or wanted to stay at her house, and she did it with no questions asked. Up next, we had Momma Quetta, may her soul now rest in peace. She didn't play any games either. Momma Quetta was straight from NYC with a big family all in one house and still she embraced us like we were hers.

Lastly, but certainly not least, we had my dear Teeny, may her soul also rest in peace. Teeny was sure to have a meal available on her stove and we were welcome to break bread with her and her kids anytime. Two of the lovely ladies, I'm sad to say, is no longer with us, the other two are still just as sweet as when I first met them and still they are only a call away.

The definition of the word intentional is something that is done on purpose or deliberately. I use that word often because it makes me understand things more clearly. When something is done with intent, that means the purpose will be revealed not too far behind it. Over the years I have learned that everything that Father Yah does is intentional and with true purpose. As I write this, the tears progressively start to flow. I didn't understand the traumatic side of things, I never even realized that what I went through was traumatic. I looked at it all as normal. Taking care of children at a young age while experiencing the loss of my own childhood can be looked at in two ways. One, I can dwell on it as if it was wrong. Or two, I can look at it from the perspective that it made me who I am today, mature and an excellent caretaker. It just seemed to flow from me naturally.

I would often use the phrase "I just did it", but technically it wasn't me doing anything because each time my mom chose to walk out the door, it was the Most High that actually covered us from danger. I have asked myself this one particular question numerous times until, in my latter days, my relationship with Father Yah became personal. It was then that I received the answer from the Ruach (Holy Spirit). The question was how could a child raise children? However, it wasn't a child that was raising children, it was Yah's grace covering us all, even in our innocence of not yet knowing Him.

It would be the year 2000, after graduating high school, that Yah's true purpose for me would soon present itself. By that point, I had formed a heart-attached relationship, at least on my end. Let's just say the guy was an on-again off-again, live-in boyfriend at the time. By live-in I mean he stayed countless nights under my mother's roof. We had been seeing each other since I was fifteen, I was now seventeen and in love. Let me just say that in my opinion, when we think of generational curses our minds tend to think of the young black males. We fail to look at young ladies who are vulnerable to repeating the cycles of a mother's life as well. So while it's safe to say that even though I didn't use drugs, nor did I mistreat my children, neither did I prostitute myself, I did fall victim to teenage love which is dopamine, a kind of pleasure hormone that acts like a drug all by itself.

After twenty-six years of my mother being in the street life and falling victim to such a strong drug, who knew, other than Father Yah, that it would end the way it did? My mother was arrested while in a drug house and was faced with serving a lot of time. Father Yah sent a compassionate judge who proposed the option of her going into rehab. That is what saved and changed her life. When Mom and I look back to that particular year, we both agree that the Judge wasn't just a judge, he was a vessel that was used by Father Yah to place her on the path to righteousness. I can speak for my mother when I say it's been twenty plus years that she's been clean. She has been married for almost twenty years now and is walking in divine favor with Father Yah. It does my heart well to see how her life has turned for the good, it's such a blessing.

Father Yah was so strategic that the timing of Mom being presented with facing jail time or rehab was perfect. I was already in a position to take custody of my brothers and as a result, they did not end up in the child endangerment system. The lesson that the Father taught me stemmed all the way back to me being a little girl. Yah had been preparing me for that very hour because He knows everything. He knew that I would need to be there to be with my brothers so that the government wouldn't take them. Now that Mom was gone on the road to recovery, she knew that they were with someone safe and who loved them. She could now focus on her healing.

There are some things that you just can't explain without having solid proof. I have carried this around with me since I was a young girl. My intent was to show my children's children.

Lesson 1
Love Shouldn't Hurt

Dear Self,

As you enter this chapter, know that you are about to be set free from the roots that still linger in the soil of your heart. This is not particularly about anyone else but you. It's ok to be selfish sometimes and this moment is that moment. This is your truth, your path, and your pain. I know you will never intentionally hurt anyone. If anything, Yah wants you to release so that you can help someone understand that if He freed you, He could free them too.

I remember this party like it was yesterday. It was a teen party that was held on Mead Street, those parties used to have the whole house jumping. It was the winter of 1997 when me and my friend, Chimere, were headed to our first house party. I was fifteen, soon to be sixteen, and Chimere was already sixteen. She was more like a sister to me. We were tight like glue and she never judged the way my home life was. If anything, she embraced that thing with me, even calling my mother Mom. I bet that's why my mom gave me a little wiggle room and let me go with her, but I was glad she did. I got to hang out and be around other kids from around the hood.

As soon as we turned the corner onto the street where the party was, all we could hear was the reggae music playing through the open windows and doors. There were a lot of kids walking in the same direction, so we knew it was going to be packed. It seemed like the party gave me some life and a nerve I didn't know I had. I found my body moving in ways I had no clue it could. I couldn't get off the dance floor that night. Song after song, I swayed with the beat that was vibrating through my ears. I danced alone and with Chimere when she wanted to. I was having a good time!

I didn't care that it was hot and sweaty in there, I only wanted to have fun with my best friend to a rhythm that moved my hips. Something about the way I jammed to the Jamaican beats grabbed the attention of someone I hadn't noticed at first. I can remember quickly turning my head around to see his face as he was tapping me on my shoulder. He directed me back to the nearest corner away from the dance floor so I could dance with him. In the middle of us dancing, he whispered in my ear, "I didn't know you dance like that."

As the night went on, me and him moved in sync. I don't even remember where Chimere was because I was enjoying myself too much. After a while, I felt like it was getting a bit late and when I checked the time it was 1 a.m. We needed to get going. I searched a little bit and found Chimere so that we could make sure to walk back home together just as our moms told us to do. She and I left the house and started walking off when he came over to hand me a piece of paper that his number was already written on. That number was like gold to me. As we were walking back to my house, like two streets over, we were so hyped. Even though Chimere and I talked about everything that had just taken place, we were sleepy at the same time. I was hyped about more than just the party and I took that number home and put it under my pillow.

It was about three days later that I finally got a chance to call him. We had made plans to meet up at his cousin's house in Fight Village projects and that's where I met him. I don't know how I got my mom to say yeah to that, but you can bet I had my brothers tagging along with me as if they were my children. As he and I were hanging out and talking, a girl came over and asked me what I was doing. At that moment it was revealed that I wasn't the only one that walked out of that party with his phone number that night. I tell you within a week's time span I was fighting that girl over him. He was my boyfriend, at least that's how I felt. But honestly, he'd just been playing the field at a young age and was good at it too. I believe that was the first red flag that Yah was giving me, but I didn't have a relationship with Him nor did I know the Most-High to even understand the warning.

A full month had gone by and I'd barely gotten to see or talk to him. As much as I wanted to, I had to wait 'til the days that Mom said I could use her phone. It was early in our acquaintance and there was still a lot I didn't know about him. What I did know was that there was a spark in the attention he'd given me at that party. He had set a fire inside of an empty little girl who was looking for just a little affection. It was him choosing me over other girls that made me feel special. I had never been the girl that boys tripped over themselves to get to, I was always the one they overlooked or the one they saw as just a friend. For him to want me as more than a friend, for him to not overlook me, was the attention I had longed for. The fire of me really liking him burned so hard within me that I started asking other kids at school, those who took the bus to his neighborhood if they knew him. And after all that hunting, I was sure to find a few things out about him. Scripture tells us to seek, and we shall find. And I did.

Eventually, we would get to talking on the phone and seeing each other a little more, that caused my feelings for him to grow even stronger. Finally, after a while, he asked me to be his girlfriend. I gladly said yes. I never asked him for honesty, but because I was truthful about everything in my life, I expected the same thing from him in return. After dating, well, what I called dating, and him coming to my house and being in the neighborhood more and more over at his cousin's house, I was sure Mom knew he was my boyfriend, but she never addressed him as such. She referred to him as my little friend, but that didn't matter to me. The more time I spent with him, the less time I was spending with my close friends. I know they started to notice but I don't recall them saying a word to me about not being around. I guess that's what happens when you get older and become preoccupied with other things like boyfriends and jobs.

It was fun being his girlfriend when he was around me, but the days I didn't get to see him was mind-boggling. I was always on edge about what he was doing or who he was with. When we were around each other, he made me feel like I was the only one in his life. Around him, I felt beautiful and like I was more than a second mom to my brothers the way I felt when I was in my own home when he wasn't around. When I was with him, I didn't feel like I had a care in the world, and if I did have any cares or concerns, he would help me with them. At sixteen years old, I had finally experienced true love. Or so I thought.

I don't recall how much time had gone by between the time we started out as boyfriend and girlfriend and the time I found myself questioning if love was supposed to love me back. All I know is that it was around that time that I would feel my first strike of real heart pain from him. That heart strike came when I found out through the grapevine that he'd gotten a girl pregnant. This was a girl he'd been with before me and by the time I learned about the pregnancy, she was four months away from giving birth to their first child. I had no clue how to handle that kind of drama.

He'd been so smooth with the fact he had a baby on the way. He never confessed out of his own mouth that his life was on the brink of a major change and my curiosity and stupidity had me waiting until the baby arrived for me to start asking questions. And when the child did arrive, there was no denying that baby. While I waited, I was still drawn to him, but once the baby arrived and I saw it, I knew he was the father. The photo of his son hurt my heart very badly. Sadly enough, him getting another girl pregnant didn't make me stop wanting him.

Down the line, I still wasn't ready to confess that I had now entered a game of Russian roulette with him. After having his first child with his first baby's mom, he then went on to cheat with another girl that lived in his neighborhood. She birthed his first daughter. Again, I waited around for the results and once that child was born, there was no denying that baby girl. What the heck was wrong with me? Why didn't I walk away? Because I stayed with him, I ended up reliving that vicious cycle. This boy that I loved went back to the mother of his first baby and got her pregnant again. This time he had another daughter. Then, as the cycle continued, he struck again, going back to the second child's mother. With her, he had another son, bringing the count to four children by the time he and I were twenty years old, two boys and two girls.

I never would have imagined accepting that kind of pain for the next six-plus years of my life, but I did just that. I accepted it. I know, I know, it's jaw-dropping. Even as I'm writing it, the hurt is reoccurring and as I look back, I cannot mentally understand why I accepted such hurt, lies, manipulation, and false love.

Having the responsibility of my brothers at such a young age let me know that I was not in the business of wanting children right away. So, when I did slip up and get pregnant at seventeen, right after graduation, I was so scared. My emotions were high, and I didn't know how to tell my mother. I knew I had a good career path ahead of me. I was fresh out of high school and didn't want to be included in what seemed to look like a race of who could have the most babies for him. All those emotions caused me to react out of fear. That fear got the best of me and the next thing I knew I was having an abortion.

Is Love Blind?

I once heard that love is blind. Well, I can attest that it is. The man that gave me the attention I longed for stole my heart and wouldn't give it back. Over the many years, the intensity of the love that I felt for him overruled the layers of hurt that he caused me. Eight years after meeting Mr. Drama, he would become my first husband. A year after getting married, we decided that was a good time to have kids together. Despite all that happened, no one could tell me that he didn't love me. We would fight like Ike and Tina and then be like Bonny and Clyde the next day. Our love was so unhealthy, and I was so broken on the inside from the constant deception and lies. But how broken was I if I kept accepting it?

When I mentioned that we would fight like Ike and Tina in the movie *What's Love Got To Do With It*, that fighting was because I didn't know how to channel my hurt and frustration. Even though I stayed in the relationship for a long time, it wasn't like I just bowed my head down and took the deception. Eventually, I would take on the role of an abuser. During many of the times, that bad news came my way, or when I found a phone number in his phone, or when he didn't come home until the next day, I would lay hands on him and not pray.

I formed a seriously bad habit of putting my hands on him out of frustration. We would fight like it was the royal rumble or something, then the next day when he would go around family and friends, they would see battle wounds on his body and quickly assume me to be the crazy one. It was so bad that the emotional abuse I was feeling on the inside would turn into physical abuse displayed on the outside. As I stated before, our long-lasting relationship and marriage was not healthy neither was it a true representation of the love that Father Yah speaks of in His Word.

Revelations were received right in the middle of me writing this book. One revelation compared the relationship that I had with my ex-husband to the relationship that we have with our Heavenly Father. We hurt him to His core when all He wants to do is show us the love that surpasses all understanding. We hurt Him to the core when all He wants to do is show that He will never leave us nor forsake us. But just like when we're in an unhealthy relationship, we continue to draw from Him and not to Him. Yah loves us so much and truly cares for us, but we leave Him with open arms and tears in His eyes, never stopping to think just how much He loves us and cares for us. We treat Him like He is a revolving door, only coming to Him when we want something.

Well, it's through my pain that I now understand that what I went through wasn't just for me. It was for a greater purpose. The Most-High presumed that I was a good candidate to endure the constant hurt and pain for the sole purpose of me knowing how He feels when we deliberately sin against Him.

He Hurts: I now know how our Father feels when we walk away from His unfailing love.

He Cries: I now know what He feels when we close the door in his face.

He Mourns: Do we think that Father Yah is not hurt by our actions, considering how we treat him? I am a true ambassador here to tell you that we must become aware of how we are treating our Heavenly Father with the choices that we make. Scripture tells us to choose this day whom you will serve (Joshua 24:15).

The lesson that Father Yah has taught me here is that feelings are real, and what makes us think that our Father who resides in Heaven does not feel the emptiness of His wandering children? I've learned that there is a possibility that love can cost us everything, or we can take our life lessons and learn to hear the message through the pain. As I write this, Yah has healed my final wound and enlarged my territory.

Lesson 2
Create the Braid: A Gift in My Hands

And I have filled him with the Spirit of YAH, in wisdom, and in understanding, and in knowledge and in all manner of workmanship— To devise cunning works, to work in gold, and in silver and in brass, and in cutting of stones, to set them, and in carving of timber to work in all manner of workmanship.

Exodus 31:3-5(SHV)

Unbraiding Your True Gifts

It's said that the early bird gets the worm and at 8:30 a.m. I got a word from the Most High.

I finished braiding Sonja's hair quickly, I thought to myself as I prepared to leave her house. Before I did, I checked around her living room to make sure all my hair supplies were packed in my bag and they were. I jumped in my car and before I knew it, I was home. It was exactly 8:55 a.m. when I arrived in my driveway. Backing in, I parked, turned the radio down, and told Father Yah, "Thank You for allowing me to make it home safely."

I reached over to grab my tote bag so that I could take it inside the house with me when I looked over to my left and saw the sun shining brightly in the sky. Beaming sunrays danced on my beautiful brown skin face. Feeling the warmth of the sun was so relaxing to my soul that I wasn't ready to go into the house just yet. I laid my head back on the headrest of the car seat and immediately thought about the crafty work I'd just done in Sonja's hair. I realized that I had a true gift, especially when I looked at the picture on my phone and saw how I'd just crocheted her hair so neatly and prettily. Remembering the details of the hidden braids that were secured underneath the crochet, I began to reminisce about when I first started braiding hair.

The Beginning

The baby dolls that Mom bought me were not in vain, I tell you! I would comb then braid, comb then braid, and keep practicing until I had perfected my craft. I would move on from the dolls to doing my own hair at thirteen years old. At that time, I was in the infancy stages of braiding techniques but felt like I was creating the work of a professional. By age sixteen, click, click, click was the sound of my bracelets clinging together as my hands were moving very quickly, braiding countless strands of hair while creating neatly parted rows. In a short time, I had built a mini clientele of friends from the neighborhood and family members that didn't live too far. I didn't even know it at the time, but the front porch of our home on Clifford Avenue was a mini hair salon.

Back then, braiding was an outlet to escape the world I lived in, a world that seemed to only pertain to adults and their needs. I became more and more passionate about my craft the more I kept braiding. I would make about twenty-five to thirty-five dollars per head. Although the dollars weren't much, it was some money in my pocket and of course, I had to make sure Mom got half of the profits. After all, she was the one supplying the hair combs and the hair grease for me to use on my clients at that time. Speaking of Mom, she is the reason I learned to braid. When she used to comb my hair, I would scoot so far down in the chair. I was trying to get away from her hands. I can still hear her saying, "Where you going?" I was trying to get away from the pain of the tension and the pulling tightly of my hair.

I cringed in the car as I reminisced on the agony I felt at those moments.

    I adored braiding hair. It brought me satisfaction seeing the creativity of the different patterns. Around the time I had started braiding, there weren't many young people in the neighborhood doing hair. Therefore, I was trying to get everybody in my kitchen chair that I'd brought outside to the porch. The older I got, the more official I was with the versatility of the braiding styles. I started getting creative and fancy with my parting patterns also known as freestyle braids. Other styles that I perfected were Iverson's, zigzag, and crisscross. I could do things like put your name in your hair and heart designs. You name it, I was at it. It didn't matter who it was, men, women, and kids were able to get their hair finessed by me.

    I didn't understand that what I was doing then was preparing me for a business. Scripture tells us that a man's gift makes room for him and brings him before great men (Proverbs 18:16 NKJV). So, I guess it's safe to say that I was destined by my heavenly Father Yah to become a licensed beauty culturist that loves the art of hairdressing. I was captivated by how fast my hands could move after separating the strands of hair into three parts and weaving them into a tightly stitched masterpiece. As I did, I allowed the braid to become finer and thinner as I neared the end of it. You couldn't tell me anything at that time. What I didn't yet know was that Yah was positioning me for a part of my destiny.

Impulsively, I jumped out of deep thought, back into my reality, and grabbed the door handle to get out of my car so that I could go into the house. But then, I heard a sweet, still, voice that said, "Be still and know that I Am Yah." And that's just what I did.

I am able to recognize His voice and I know that when Father Yah speaks, I must listen. I sat quietly a little while longer only to embrace the arresting spirit of quietness. I heard the voice again that lets me know, "I have placed the gift in your hands. As each strand of hair that you touch begins to interlock, I Am weaving My grace along with it. Know that each client you have encountered has been sent by Me."

As the tears started to flow, I began to yell, "Thank You, Yah, for Your faithfulness and unfailing love!" The silence that was once in the car was no more. I was sure my family in the house and my neighbors could hear me worshiping in the car. I didn't care! Those breakthrough moments are vital to my healing. It just so happened to be in the car that day.

I write this book with the intent to tell pieces of my story while making sure the Most High remains the center of the glory for what He has done in my life. You will notice the intertwining of many physical and spiritual gifts and opportunities that have been pursued and some completed. I ask that you allow me to be the vessel that will remind you to never let others define who you are and point you toward knowing your worth when it comes to the Heavenly Father, Yah. Throughout these lessons that you will read, I hope they inspire you to never be afraid to make mistakes and grow.

Heavenly Father,

We praise You for the many gifts and the talents that You continue to bless us with. For just as You supplied the children of Israel on their journey in biblical times, it has now flowed into the current moments. For I believe that every person has some skill, talent, or ability that singles them out as gifted and unique. For You have given us a Comforter who aids us innumerable possibilities. We also praise You for being faithful to all Your promises. You have ensured us in knowing that not a word of Your promises fall to the ground or returns void. When men seek to obstruct Your plans, You turn the evil and make things good. Teach us to find confidence in Your prepared plans for our lives. For we know those whom Yah chooses, He will direct their path even if it takes numerous years.

Together we all agree and say Amen.

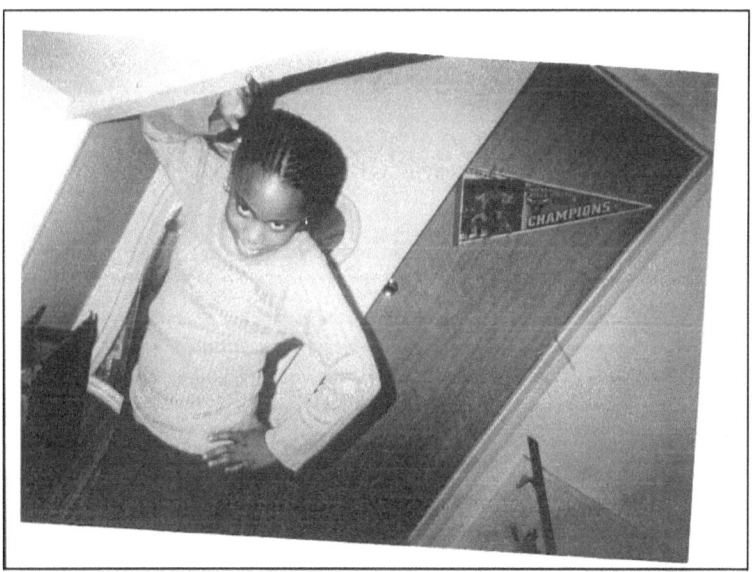

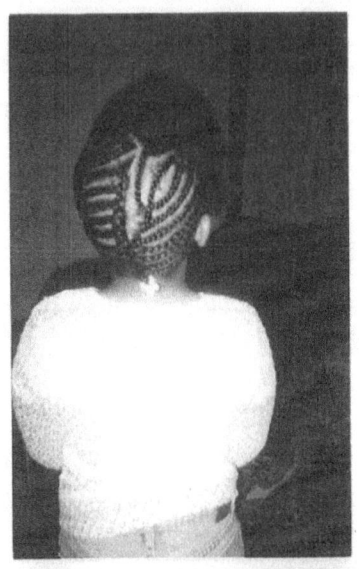

Pictures bring everything into focus for me. Here is proof of my work at such a young age I was braiding her hair. The little girl in the photo is Alexis Harvey. At the release of this book, she was 29-years old.

Lesson 3
Unbraiding the Fight of Wickedness

For we wrestle not against flesh and blood, but against principalities, against powers, against the rulers of the darkness of this world, against spiritual wickedness in high places.

Ephesians 6:12 (KJV)

The time was 11:39 p.m. on a Friday, let's just call it a family movie night, something we'd decided to do when we could. I looked around to see that everyone had fallen asleep on me, which was strange because I was usually the one that fell asleep first. I laughed while saying to myself, "Wait 'til the morning when I show them this picture I've taken of them sleeping." I had to take the picture because every time I'd gone to sleep first, they seemed to always catch me slipping.

I turned the television off, making sure to cover them all up, then I grabbed my blanket and hopped back in my spot to get comfortable. I grabbed my phone and went straight to my social media account to stroll and see what others had going on that night. As I scrolled, I realized that not much was happening. But as I was swiping up to move the thread along, I came across a video of some girls talking loudly and proceeding to fight. I was quick to make sure that I turned my volume down, I didn't want to wake my family.

I continued to watch the video and when I had taken a second to think about it I thought there was something odd about it. Usually, whenever I came across fights, I scrolled past them because I always found something so distasteful when I saw people taking the time to film a fight. It made me wonder who in the world just stood there videoing people fighting instead of breaking it up? But as I watched a little more of the video, I heard someone in the background yelling, "That girl don't bother nobody. And now look, they bullied her 'til she got tired of it." That's all I needed to hear to take me deep in thought to the time I was being bullied.

Before I knew it, I lay my head back and was relaxed on the couch, drifting into deep thoughts about when I was in high school being bullied. I'd had that same experience of not bothering anybody but was picked as a target to be bullied. I wondered what was it about me that made her think I was a pushover? The more I thought about school-aged kids, the more frustrated I became until I said to myself, "Kids can be so rude and mean."

I can remember coming across this article one day that pointed out some of the reasons why bullies are the way they are. Some of the data said that bullies are cowards with no real courage. They generally prey on those who are weaker and more vulnerable than they are. They also have been known to demean some, eager to prove their power and superiority to others. And finally, the major factor for a bully's behavior can be the lack of love!

When I think back, I can see how they may have assumed I was weaker and vulnerable. As a first-year student, I didn't have the latest gear or shoes, which didn't matter much to me since I just wanted to mind my business and do my work. My Payless shoes weren't bothering anybody. I was very standoffish and unaware that my social skills were lacking. I'm sure a lot of that had to do with me being around a bunch of people I didn't know and hadn't yet built relationships with. That still didn't give them the right to try to gain power at my expense.

I can remember two particular bullies that made me their targets.

Bully Number One - *Big Bertha!*

When I dreamed of going to high school, I certainly didn't dream of bullies being there. Having to worry about my wardrobe being approved and accepted by others was so far off. I was sixteen years old and trying to get acclimated to reading schedules and remembering locker codes, not picking my pencil and books off the floor every time Big Bertha decided she wanted to walk past and knock them off my desk. If my memory served me right, each time she did it I just wanted to slap her, but I didn't think little ole me could handle her. Big Bertha was tall and heavy and looked strong. I didn't think there was any way I could take her on.

One day I went to school and I was feeling very prideful about how I looked. Me and my best friend Candice, who attended a different school, had made plans the night before to wear a similar outfit. We had both gotten these t-shirts with our names printed on the back of them. Candice's shirt was purple, mine was red, and we both wore black leggings. It's funny as I think back to my shoes, they were called Eastsides or something like that and they were from Payless while Candice wore her Jordans. But that didn't bother me, I was feeling myself. That was my first shirt with my name on the back of it.

But noooo! Big bertha played a major part in knocking that pride down and quickly. She had her friends look over at my non-named brand shoes and they all had a humorous time laughing at me. Suddenly, the feeling of just wanting to go home came over me and that was weird because school was always my outlet to get away from the responsibilities of home life. Her messing with me didn't go on too much longer. On this particular day, I was fed up with how she teased me. I had reached a point where I made up my mind that I was not going to allow it to keep going on. The bullying had to stop. Either way, I was going to make a decision that would let her know how I felt. I didn't care how I was going to get my point across, she was going to find out.

After third-period class, we were walking down the hall, headed to lunch, when she tried to trip me, but I caught my balance. A few of the kids that saw what she did laugh while some asked me if I was okay. If looks could kill she would have been slain at that moment. I had given her a stare that said I was extremely tired of her foolishness. *Big Bertha* was in for a rude awakening when we arrived next to the *exit 3* stairwells.

I said, "You want to fight? I'm tired of you!"

She snarled her face up and said, "Let's go!"

Some of the kids who were already heading to lunch started yelling, "Fight! Fight! Fight!" as we headed to the bottom of the steps.

She was on one side of the stairwell, and I was on the other. It was like we were headed to a boxing ring. There were kids standing all around, waiting to see who was going to get beat down that day. For me, I didn't care if I was going to get my behind whooped, I just wanted to be left alone after that. I felt that if I at least stood up to her, she would know I wasn't afraid of her and to back up off me.

My adrenaline was pumping because I was scared. It was my first time fighting and I didn't know if I could or not. I was going to see if my thoughts of how to fight would pay off or let me down. All types of stuff were going through my brain at that moment. I can remember thinking that she was bigger than me, probably about two hundred thirty pounds. I was weighing in at maybe one hundred-thirty. Oh, well. It was either her or me. One or both of us were going to feel some pain.

Big Bertha stepped toward me and it was on. I don't recall who threw the first punch but I know I ended that fight with her shirt over her head and her against the wall just getting pounded on. It was like the strength I had came out of nowhere. The yells of the kids drew the attention of the adults but the loudest noise I heard was my heart beating in my ear. I couldn't believe I was fighting my own fears. I was fighting to be free from the troubles that fear brought me. I was fighting to prove to myself that I could defeat anything that I no longer wanted in my life. While throwing blow after blow, I became proud of myself for facing my fears.

As staff and others came to break up the fight, I heard someone say, "You better not mess with her, that's a girl Tyson." Even though I heard them say that, I was too emersed with relief that I got some bottled-up frustration out, not only from Bertha violating my personal space numerous of times but from just growing up in my home situation. That alone was more pressure than I could handle.

After that fight, Bertha didn't bother me anymore. I do recall her rolling her eyes when she would see me, but she didn't touch my things or say a single word to me. I'm sure she probably found another target, but after standing up to her, I didn't have to deal with her mess anymore. For that matter, I didn't have to deal with anybody bothering me for the rest of my freshman year of high school. It seemed as though I had set a standard of not being the one to be messed with even though I was quiet and shy, at least in school. I remember getting home and explaining to my mother how it all started. She didn't get upset because she knew that to make me fight and get suspended from school, someone had to really be bothering me.

During my childhood and early teens, I still hadn't formed a personal relationship with Father Yah. Yet unbeknownst to me, He had always been there for me. Now that I know My Heavenly Father, I'm reminded of the story in the bible of David and Goliath.

David was a young Israelite shepherd boy who knew that he was from a chosen generation. When it came to his stature, he was skinny and not big with muscles. He wasn't trained for the battlefield like the strong soldiers were, but David knew divinely that the Most-High would keep him and protect him through the challenge of standing up to that giant. None of the Israelite soldiers who were strong and mighty had the courage and boldness that David did in that very hour. Standing up to that giant gave David a new life, he became a champion over the Philistines whom he had defeated by killing the giant.

I'm so grateful that I was able to share that story because it gave me a clear understanding of the fight I had with Big Bertha. Although the situation was tough, Father Yah gave me the strength to stand up for myself, to be bold, and to fight back. I didn't yet know that He was my protector through uncertain times in my life.

Bully Number Two - *Whole Lotta*!

Whole Lotta was the bus bully who, again, was big in size and had an entourage of friends all from the same neighborhood. I don't ever recall seeing her too much in school. I don't know why she didn't like me or what drew her to become a bully to me. Keeping to myself, I very rarely did anything to draw attention. I hated having to worry about kids on the school bus wanting to "try me". At sixteen years old, my focus was on my grades and my responsibilities at home. The kids on the bus seemed to catch a thrill from throwing their weight and strength around and showing off for each other. Even though I had fought in school already, I wasn't that confident to think I could just go on fighting the world.

I remember when they got on the bus at the corner of Conkey and Clifford Ave. They would all get on deep, and out of all of them, it seemed that *Whole Lotta* would always hit somebody as she walked down the aisle to get to the back of the bus. You never knew who she was going to hit. Some of the kids knew her and may have said words back to her, however, I was a quiet homebody. I did hear that if you lived on that street or near it you were known to be rough and tough and didn't take any mess. I didn't know them personally. I didn't get around to playing with other kids much unless you lived across the street from me or next door. I didn't know any of the kids from that area, which I was okay with. They didn't seem like the type of kids I wanted to be friends with anyway.

My first encounter with this bully was her mushing my head as she passed by my seat. By "mushing" I mean she used the palm of her hand to push my head. I brushed it off and shook my head to myself in disgust. I didn't respond in a threatening manner because I didn't want to fight, again. I knew I could fight if I had to, but I didn't feel I had to at that moment.

Whole Lotta picked and chose who she wanted to bother and on that particular day she decided that she was going to target me for the second time to many. Boarding the bus to go home, I found a seat directly in the middle of the. When Whole Lotta boarded, she proceeded to the back of the bus where she would always sit, her and her friends. As she headed toward that spot in the back, she mushed my head against the back of the seat. That time it was done with some force. Well, I didn't say anything to her, again. If I would have, it was a strong possibility that I would have gotten jumped by her and her friends. Plus, the area on the bus was too confined.

I remained in my seat by myself with tears in my eyes and anger flooding my emotions. I was a kid that only wanted to go home, go to school, get good grades, help my mom, and just live my life. Constantly being bullied was changing me in ways that I didn't want. I was never as angry before the bullying began. The other instance of being picked on started replaying in my mind. Each time a moment came up, more anger came with it. Not even halfway home yet, I suddenly had premeditated murder on my mind. It wasn't until we got to our stop at the corner of Conkey and Clifford Ave that from that day forward I would have to change my bus route.

We got off the bus and I didn't even let it pull off before I turned around and started to throw left and right hooks. I continuously allowed them to connect right with her face. Thinking about the hurt she caused me and others added more fuel to the fight in me. Like my first fight, I didn't want to, but I had no choice. If I was ever going to be free from my fears of bullies, I had to show them that I wasn't the one to mess with. I don't know how long we fought, but I remember a stranger finally breaking us apart and telling us to stop fighting. Breathing heavily, I looked at her being held up by a few of her friends. No one held me up. No one checked to make sure I was okay. No one yelled to go get my mother. No one comforted me like they were doing with her.

As it turned out, I had beaten her up so badly that her best friend wanted to fight me. She wasn't at the fight but had heard about it as everyone else did. We never did fight, but I knew I had to watch out for myself. I had my mom contact the school to change my bus stop or I would have to prepare to fight every day. After that, I never had to fight any one of them again because I didn't go down that way often, and neither did I see the troublemakers in school. As time went on, I had a few fights with kids on the street but would become friends with them again after. There was something about my personality that made it so that as long as people didn't bother me or disrespect my personal space, I was ok. But the minute anyone did cross my lines, I would then go into attack mode. I had underlying anger issues and didn't realize it at that time.

Heavenly Father,

I come to you praying for myself and the reader. Just want to thank You for not leaving us defenseless when coming into battle against the enemy and his wickedness. At one point in our lives we had no full understanding that You have prepared everything we need to live a life of godliness. You are a generous and caring Father who wants to protect and equip us with exactly what we need to fight against the enemy. I pray with an urgency for those that are lost and desire to be found. I pray that they will learn to put on the spiritual armor that You have provided. Help us to not rely on our own armor. Allow us to pursue the weapons of righteousness and truth so that we can stand firm in your Word and not our own inadequate strength. For You continually make a way of escape for those that belong to You. As we read this, we are coming together in agreement that you will fight our battles as we give them over to you. -Amen.

Lesson 4
It's A Man's World

Welcome to another day in the life of mommy hood, where you're off your nine-to-five job, only to be at work in your home. Being a mom is an around-the-clock job that Yah has blessed me with. At times I need a break, but I wouldn't trade it for anything.

Dear Sons,

"As I watch you grow up and move into your teenage years, it is Imperative I tell you that you can do whatever you want to do in this thing called life. Don't let anyone tell you what you can't do or what you can't be."

Often, hubby or I check in with our oldest son to see how he's doing and how he is feeling all while making sure to pay strong attention to his body language. Due to me being an active parent leader in the community I live in, I know that mental health is real and that teens face a lot of temptation these days. Social media and social ideas can take their toll on the minds of teens. So, the key goal in our house is to create a space to make the kids feel comfortable and safe if they need to talk to us. We're also big on making sure that the Word of Yah is in them as they all continue to grow so quickly.

It was around 11:00 a.m. on a Saturday, the two younger boys were out running some errands with dad, and I expected them to be out for about two hours. That left me with more than enough time to talk to the oldest and have a little quiet time for myself. One part of my plan was to do something silly to set the tone for me and him to talk openly. I burst into his room abruptly like something was wrong. I startled him as he played the video game. He looked over at me to see if everything was ok. We stared at each other for a few minutes, then broke into enjoyable laughter. The other part of the plan was to purposely disrupt him from being preoccupied with the video game. The look on his face was priceless when he saw me laughing.

All he could do was shake his head and say, "Really, Mom?" I humorously opened the conversation by reminding him that he didn't have long before he would officially be out of high school and considered an adult. We both laughed at the idea of him being out on his own. My laughter insinuated that there was a big world waiting for him out there while he laughed and added, "Yea, I can't wait." As soon as he said that, my whole mood switched. As a parent, you always want to make sure your kids are ready for the cares of life that are headed their way.

I was confused about what happened to my emotions. I went from joking with him straight into mommy mode. I gently grabbed his face with both hands, making sure to look him in his eyes. Tears began to roll down my face as I calmly, but sternly told him, "Never let anyone tell you what you can't be, or better yet, never let someone talk you out of your dreams."

He looked back up at me and said, "I know, Mom. I won't." I then reached over and gave him the biggest hug a mother could give her firstborn son while also letting him know that I loved him.

Walking out of his room, I began to feel my emotions rising. I went straight to my room and plopped across the bed. It seemed like when I made that statement about never letting anyone talk him out of his dreams, my energy went low and my mind went straight to a memory where I'd allowed that very thing to happen to me. Thinking back to the moments leading up to when my dreams were shattered by someone else's words caused heaviness in my heart.

As I'd started my approach to becoming a young adult, around my last years of high school, the excitement of graduation was right there. I knew that I had some pretty neat things ahead of me as far as a career path was concerned. I was about to graduate from Edison Technical and Career High School in Rochester NY. I realize now how much the teachers thrived on the chance to provide as many urban students as possible with the opportunity to invent their own futures. There was very little wiggle room which meant there was very little room to fail. They made sure to provide us with mentorship, internships, and counselor support to meet our needs of excelling in the technical trades and careers that were offered. At that age, though, I didn't understand the skill trades and opportunities that were right before me.

Just to give a little back story, when a student arrived in their freshman year of high school at Edison, they were given numerous shop-focused classes to explore, which I think was brilliant. It allowed them to see multiple options before minimizing it down to two or three selections on what career path they wanted to lean toward. The final pick of their number one choice was left to the counselor. Then, leading into their tenth-grade year, they started to pursue the career path they and the school had chosen. Well, I followed all the steps above. The only thing was that I didn't get my first or second choice of trade path.

I can remember the two options I chose. They were cosmetology because I loved to do hair and daycare because I was good at taking care of kids. Well, my wish was not granted. I was placed in welding and construction class. Something told me that Father Yah was up to something and that He had a hand in that placement. Not only did I feel that it was a mix-up, but I felt out of place. I was the only female in the welding class. After going to my counselor about the mix-up, they somehow convinced me to wait until the next semester before opting out of it. Well, guess what? Throughout that time, I began to take a liking to it.

Fast forward to 2000, my senior year, and things were lining up for me. I was feeling energetic about becoming the first young, brown skin welder. I had the support of so many counselors and mentors who saw the opportunities and the potential that was in me. To be honest, it's because of them and the constant push for me, that I got as far as I did. Truly, I didn't understand what was ahead in my future, but I felt empowered by those that motivated me. I will never forget them. I had Mr. Scott, Mr. Patterson, Mr. Baker, and Mrs. Iglesias. All were dedicated, not just to me but to all youth that came their way.

One of the things that were mandatory for the shop program was participation in an internship and completing a certain number of hours before graduating. I was so blessed with the opportunity to do mine at the City of Rochester Department of Environmental Services as a welder's aid. I absorbed so much information and techniques while experiencing the real-life workforce. I was told by the program supervisor that the job was mine and waiting for me after graduation. I did everything required to make sure I was off to the best start possible in adulthood. I had completed numerous training courses to add to my resume and expertise. I also made sure to get all I could from whoever was there to assist me.

I have held on to these items to always have physical proof of where I've been in my life. Although I wasn't successful in pursuing that career, I'll always have proof of *Herstory* (History).

When referencing the word of Yah, scripture tells us, "...and with all thy getting get understanding (Proverbs 4:7 KJV). But when we reference it to life, we have to know that in all of our getting of information we need to make sure that we get a full understanding of what we are obtaining. Finally, graduation had arrived and brought with it job offers from other companies. I was walking into my future ready and was enjoying it.

Without warning, a sickness came over me and sleepiness. At work one day, going off a hunch, I found out I was pregnant. Scared and confused at the same time, me and my boyfriend, who would later become my first husband, scrambled to figure out what to do. I can remember his words through that process, "I don't want you working around all those men. You shouldn't be there." That very moment was when the seeds of doubt and deception were planted in my head.

The Lesson: Words Have Power

Trust in the Lord *with all your heart, and do not lean on your own understanding. In all your ways acknowledge him, and he will make straight your paths.*

Proverbs 3:5-6 ESV

After hearing my boyfriend's opinion, the next thing I knew I was telling myself that it was a man's field, and I didn't belong there. I made the decision to walk away from the path that I deeply feel Father Yah had laid out for me to take. Not only did I not keep the job, but I also didn't keep the baby. But I kept the relationship that was full of insecurities and the control that clouded my judgment for many years to follow.

Reflecting on it now makes me think about the story at the beginning of the Bible when the serpent whispered in Eve's ear. He planted the seed of deception that would change the entire path or trajectory of the world once she acted on the deception.

The path of life never stopped, but it did become harder and longer to reach a stable point in life. I never took the time to stop and understand what happened, I just moved forward chasing after the beat of my heart and my blinded eyes.

Suddenly, as the truth of my memory faded, I heard a voice call out, "Mom, what are you doing in there?" I then came out of my deep thoughts and realize that it was my son calling me. I hollered into the other room, "Nothing. Just laying down."

With the memory finally back to the past from which it came, I then hollered again, "Never let anyone talk you out of your dreams, son."

Thus says the LORD: "Stand by the roads, and look, and ask for the ancient paths, where the good way is; and walk in it and find rest for your souls. But they said, 'We will not walk in it.'

Jeremiah 6:16 ESV

And still, real-life childhood trauma had not been identified yet.

I have held on to these items to always have physical proof of where I've been in my life. Although I wasn't successful in pursuing that career, I'll always have proof of Herstory (History).

Lesson 5
Unbraiding Insight into The Blood of The Lamb

Pulmonary Embolism

I arrived at my doctor's appointment for my annual physical to ensure I was healthy as could be. Four minutes after signing in and being led to the exam room, I lay my head back on the examination bed to rest. I heard a knock of urgency at the door and quickly sit back up to see that it was the nurse. She told me that the doctor was running behind due to an emergency and he would be right in.

I told I her, "No worries. I'll sit tight."

I thank Yah for teaching me how to have patience, something I didn't always have. I lay my head back for the second time and my mind went deep into thought. Lying down brought me back to the feelings I'd had about thirteen years prior as I waited helplessly in the emergency room for the doctor to let me know what was happening to me.

The Clots that Caused Chaos

In 2009 I was twenty-seven years old and it was my second time ever riding on an airplane. I was nervous but extremely excited at the same time. I was nervous because I had never traveled alone with my three-year-old son. It was a six-hour flight that included a layover. The excitement was from leaving the cold February weather in Rochester to feel the warmth of Florida sunshine. While packing our bags and boarding the plane, I decided that the goal was to enjoy some family time with the in-laws and then get right back home. It wasn't until we landed that I realized we must be very careful about what we ask for.

It was so hot in Florida that I found it almost hard for me to enjoy myself. The sun beat down on me like a drum. I would wake up hot and sweating and then go to sleep the same. Spending time with family, enjoying dinners and having great talks made the trip memorable, but the pool was my best friend for those few days. I loved being able to go swimming whenever I wanted. When my family wanted to leave the house to do other things, I chose to stay behind. They would take my son with them, which was good because I could swim without worrying about him around the water, water that cooled my skin and lowered my temperature. I wasn't hard to please at all, just being able to have some rest and relaxation away from home was good enough for me.

Florida's heat was different from Rochester's summers. The air in Florida was so thick it could be cut with a knife, but I still loved it and would've taken the heat over the cold any day. I was enjoying my stay so much that it seemed like those four days went by quickly. I felt as if it was time well spent and before I knew it, we were headed back home on the plane. As we landed, I remember standing up and waiting in line to get off the plane. I grabbed my chest because of a sudden and abrupt pain that hit me on the left side.

Jokingly, I said to myself, "I hope I'm not having a heart attack." When the pain didn't become any worse, I went on about my day, not really thinking too much about that first sign of something being wrong.

As the days went on, the chest pain that I'd complained of at the airport would become more severe. The more I talked or moved, the more challenging it became to breathe properly. When my mother started to see the pain and agony I was having, she began to worry. Mom would constantly come in the room to check on me and prop my pillows. From that point, because of the look of concern in my mother's eyes, I knew something had to be wrong.

I became a bit fretful, thinking I was going to die. I'd never felt that type of pain in my body and I just wanted to get to the bottom of what was happening to me. So, I made sure to call my doctor who got me in to see her right away. During the exam, she gave me the normal prompts as she repeatedly told me to breathe in and out while she checked my body for the symptoms I had reported earlier. She asked if I'd taken any new medications as she looked at my chart. I was only taking birth control pills at that time. I was a healthy young lady as far as anything medical was concerned.

According to her check-up, there was nothing wrong with me, everything seemed to be normal. She told me to just go home and get some rest, she didn't offer me any meds or comfort or care instructions. But she made sure to give me the infamous instructions that all doctors give. "If anything gets worse, please notify me and you can come back in to be seen." Welp, as expected, I listened to the doctor who seemed to know best.

I went home after that and really did try to get the rest she recommended. That's when I realized I couldn't even lie down without becoming breathless. I was only able to find a little relief from pain when I was propped up with multiple pillows in the upward position. At that point, it had been three days into me feeling uncomfortable. Eventually, I could no longer stand the pain. My Aunt Karen just so happened to be around and she saw the distress I was feeling. Immediately, she drove me to the emergency room.

Once I arrived at the hospital, I sat in the waiting room with severe chest pain for almost an hour before my mother, who was with me, finally went to tell the person at the front desk the severity of my symptoms. Before I knew it, they were taking me back to be treated and seen. Per standard protocol, they asked me so many questions. Some of the questions were about travel, medications, and, of course, the chest pain. I described the pains I'd been having since returning from my trip three days prior. Immediately, I was required to take an electrocardiogram test, also known as an EKG.

An EKG records the heart's electrical activity. When there is a blood clot near the heart, the heart must work harder to circulate the blood. That blood clot can sometimes be detected by an EKG. My EKG results showed that I had a massive pulmonary embolism, which is a blood clot in the lungs. I was immediately placed on blood-thinning medication and hospitalized for five days while receiving multiple procedures and treatments.

My doctors determined that my clot was likely caused by the deep veins of my legs during air travel. The doctor made sure to explain that when you're sitting still in a confined space for a long period of time, the longer you are immobile, the greater your risk of developing a blood clot. And due to the use of birth control, the clot had to have started in my legs and then traveled all the way up to my heart and into my lungs. I was mere moments away from death and would have died had I not gone to that hospital.

The Lesson in the Clots

Prior to my experience, I had never heard of blood clots. I was unfamiliar with the signs and symptoms, so I didn't think anything much of the chest pains I'd had in the days leading up to my hospitalization. As I reflected on that very moment, the Ruach (Holy Spirit) let me know that Yah's timing was perfect timing. He allowed me to travel many miles away from home and then return home to safety before my Spiritual blood transfusion could even take place. Father Yah was arresting me so that He could purify my blood flow. It's the Passover that's the symbolic meaning for me. The Lamb that was slain was without a blemish. It's the pure and Holy blood of Yahshua (Jesus) that saves us and sets us free. This is the same blood that was put on the doorpost connecting the blood to Calvary.

It wasn't my time to die. Father Yah allowed me to understand that it wasn't my time, but He did need my attention. There was a process that needed to take place. He had to strip me to humble me and align me with His will for my life. I will forever be thankful to Yah for finding ways to save my life for His glory.

Remembering that time, with tears flowing from my eyes and a mouth filled with praise, I sat up and came back to reality. Sitting on the examination bed, I jumped off it and said, "Thank you, Father," loudly. I was so loud that the nurse knocked on the door and stuck her head in to ask me if everything was ok. I looked over at her and joyfully replied, "Yes, it is." I told her, "I'm just grateful to be alive and in good health seeing as what my body has been through in the past years."

What may sound strange to you but familiar to me is that the nurse actually came into the room, closed the door, and begin to rejoice along with me. To this day, I must say, that was one of the best doctor's appointments of my life.

The lesson I received from that situation in my life was that our timing is not the Most- High's timing. For He knows the thoughts that He has for us even when we have no clue as to what is going on. Often, we are told to trust the process of whatever He is doing and that's just what we must do. At times, what we go through can seem like the same situation someone else is going through. However, we must never forget that our journey isn't like anyone else's, therefore, we can't expect our processes to be similar.

These are biblical teachings from Romans 5:3-5 (ESV). I sum those scriptures up as suffering produces endurance, endurance produces character, and character produces hope. We simply put all our issues and problems in His hands. By doing so, we are given the strength to not give up. Not giving up builds us into what He called us to be and to do. And finally, as we are built up, we must have hope that Yah will do well with us. Hope leads us to trust in Him, but while trusting Him, we should always stay in His perfect will so that it won't be too difficult for Him to find us when the shifting comes.

As I look back to that near-death experience, I don't remember praying much or giving Yah the Glory because I didn't have a conscience to pray my way through. I was just living and giving Him thanks' here and there. What I did know, however, was that I had some people praying for me in that season, Aunt Karen was definitely one. I know she was praying because there were times that she would call me and I would be down and out. In the midst of us talking, she would stop all conversation and begin to pray. I'm so glad she prayed for me.

Although I never doubted that Father Yah was keeping me, I can remember how grateful I felt when I replayed the situation in my head. The more I thought about it, the more I realized that I could have been stuck in a Florida hospital with no familiar doctors while worrying about my son. But my sickness was intentional, so intentional that Yah knew my healing would lead me directly to Him. He set me up good and I didn't even get that revelation until my life was In His perfect peace.

> *Exodus 12:13 (KJV). And the blood shall be to you for a token upon the houses where ye are: and when I see the blood, I will pass over you, and the plague shall not be upon you to destroy you, when I smite the land of Egypt.*

> *Isaiah 53:5 (KJV). But He was wounded for our transgressions, He was bruised for our iniquities; The chastisement for our peace was upon Him, And by His stripes, we are healed."*

Heavenly Father,

I come to You on behalf of Your children who have been redeemed by the blood of Your precious Son Yahshua (Jesus). We ask that You forgive us for our selfish ways and that You keep us safe as we dwell in a world filled with evil. For just as You signed Your name on the hearts of the children of Israel and covered each doorpost, we share the remnant of that sacrificial Lamb's blood. In return, You have access to what we want and need through Your precious Son. We are called to be faithful to the point of death so that we can receive the eternal reward that has already been prepared for those that love and trust You. I pray that those who desire to know You more learn to lean on You're understanding and not their own. Allow us to not become discouraged when we are faced with life-changing events, but instead, let us find the peace that perfectly lies in You. Amen.

Lesson 6
Unbraiding The Joy on The Other Side of The Pain

It's not often that we stay out late as a family, we're usually in the house by eight p.m. On this one night, due to the huge fan base that WrestleMania draws in, it took us some time to get through the people and all the traffic in our local downtown. I'm not a big fan of wrestling but I watch with my family who loves the entertainment side of it. I knew they must've be exhausted from all the yelling and cheering they did that night.

We arrived home a bit after eleven Saturday night. As soon as we pulled into the driveway and got the garage door opened, I laughed as I watched all three of the boys and the husband disperse to see who could get to the bathroom first. I thought it was quite funny to watch whoever didn't make it, yell from the other side of the door, "Hurry up!"

Wrestling has a segment where the wrestlers tag teamed each other. Together, my husband and I tag-teamed things around the house. The load is not just on one person. I simply adored that we worked together and not against each other. He'd decided to take the boys upstairs and help prepare them for bed while I washed up the little dishes that we had left in the sink from earlier. The plan was for me to go straight upstairs to prepare for bed when I got done.

It didn't take long to get right into the motion of making fresh dishwater. As I proceeded to start washing the dishes, the aroma overtook me. Just to let you know, the scent of Clorox bleach infused in the dishwater screamed fresh and clean to me.

I was working on my plan to finish up the dishes so that I could get myself prepared for bed along with the rest of my family. As I was in my zone, the water was running and I was jamming to my worship music that pumped out from the speaker on my phone. I had learned that music could be therapeutic. As my hands were immersed in the water, I got poked pretty good by a knife. Immediately, I pulled my hand out and began to shake it in an up-and-down motion. Wow, that little poke really hurt! I then examined my finger and noticed that there was a little cut that needed some attention.

I stepped back from the sink to get a paper towel to dry my hand. I checked again to make sure there was no blood. All of a sudden, I practically flung my tired body against the counter, rested my elbows on the countertop, and went right into deep thought. I told y'all that Father Yah has a way of arresting my spirit right where I am. The knife and the water sparked something in me, but this particular song that had started to play really opened me up emotionally just that fast. Gracefully Broken by Tasha Cobbs started playing. The opening verse says, "Take all I have in these hands and multiply." That is the song that I kept on repeat when I surrendered my life to Yahshua (Jesus). I was Gracefully Broken.

No one was downstairs but me. I had just a little time to myself, time used to tune out any and everything at that moment. My mind took me back to the year 2009 when my world had just come crashing down. That moment in time caused me to lift my hands and surrender my life over to the Heavenly Father. Even though I disliked going back and reminiscing about those hurtful emotions, that moment allowed you, the reader, to see me in a vulnerable place, to experience the path of pain I journeyed on to get to this place of healing, peace, and joy.

The Message

January of 2009, I stood in the kitchen of my two-bedroom apartment with tears of fury in my eyes. I had to make the hard decision to end my first marriage. For good. We had separated many times before but we always seemed to finagle our way back together each time. But after over fifteen years of deception and hurt, there was going to be no more finagling. It had gotten to the point where I felt that I would take my life or his. Out of all those years of arguments and fights, I'd never felt the way I did at that moment. I had exposed my heart to him for the last time.

The girl he was cheating with at that time had the audacity to send me a text message with a picture of a baby that belonged to him and her. I can remember like it was yesterday, opening my phone to a message from an unknown number and reading the words: *THIS IS HIS BABY!* All of a sudden, at that very moment, it felt like my soul had left my body. I believe that was the exact instant I died inside.

The enemy whispered to me, "Whatever you chose to do, it would be justifiable by insanity."

As I reached my hand in the sink for the knife, I tried to walk toward him but my feet wouldn't move. At that moment I heard another voice, one that was still and small, and it said, "Vengeance is mine!"

I put the knife down and just cried. He walked out of the door at that very moment, only to be seen some weeks later. There wasn't anything new about him walking out the door and leaving me to figure things out for myself. We were already separated to the point where he felt he could come and go whenever he pleased. I hadn't even lived in the apartment I was in that long. I could count on my hands the number of times he'd come to spend a few nights or to see me and his son. He was so disconnected from us that he had no clue what troubles I was already facing. I'd never had an issue with taking care of myself or him, but things became a bit real when I had a child and took on all those extra responsibilities. The nerve of him to have a new baby.

Earlier that month, I had been served with an eviction notice. It read that the marshals were coming to dispose of all my belongings due to my lack of rent payments. Shortly after that, I found out that the head gasket in my car had blown which left me without a car, and all of this went on while I was working at my job part-time. I lay on the living room floor feeling hopeless, lost, confused, defeated, empty, and ready to give up. Everything had fallen apart in my life. I wasn't sure what I had done to get there, but things spiraled downhill fast.

Becoming a divorced woman wasn't in my life's plan. Raising our son and creating a life together was what I envisioned. However, the constant lies, the constant cheating, and the constant number of children born to him but not me had finally taken its toll. I was left many nights crying myself to sleep and many mornings waking up alone. I often questioned what I could have done wrong or what I had not done enough of to cause him to treat me so wrong. Unable to find that answer, I came to the conclusion that there wasn't anything I could do to rectify the situation.

I needed Yah and I needed Him fast. The only place I knew to find Him was at the church, so that's what I ran back to. I didn't like the feeling of emptiness I was experiencing. I wanted a quick fix from Yah like I'd gotten before, but that wasn't happening at that time. The tears were in the process of watering my future. Yah was doing a new thing in me and it didn't require my help. I felt Him working in me from the very moment I cried on that kitchen floor and said the words, "I surrender." Up to that point, that was something I had never done. I told the Father to take the keys to my soul, I couldn't drive anymore.

The leaders of the church I ran back to knew me well because they were my spiritual parents. Pastor J. Simmons and First Lady J. Simmons will always share a place in my heart. When I came back this time, after being gone for about four years, they embraced me and the tears I shed while welcoming me back with open arms. They were the vessels I needed in that particular time of my despair. Together, they assisted in the structuring of my foundation for the newness that was ahead for me. They wasted no time putting me straight to work in ministry with the kids.

While back at church, it wasn't long before I came to learn that trying to be so private about my living situation almost caused me to miss my blessing. Pastor and I were talking one day and I went to spilling my business, telling him about me facing an eviction. Little did I know, the ram in the bush was right there. After I'd told him everything, Pastor looked at me and said, "One of my apartments will be available soon. Just give me time to get it ready." Both Pastor and First Lady were heaven sent.

Father Yah knew I needed to see what integrity and structure in a family looked like and they were the perfect example. Yah was preparing me for my second husband that I didn't even see coming, but First Lady knew. When I went to tell her that we wanted to get married, she already knew because Father Yah had revealed it to her. The work of being my wedding Planner was done with such grace by her. I couldn't thank her enough.

I remember when I started to regain my strength and was feeling more empowered. I was appointed to be one of the speakers for the Women's Day service that was held the annually. The title of my message was "God Loves A Broken Vessel". As I was preparing my message the night before, I received pure revelation about where my life was and who could and would get the glory when we surrendered all to the Father. My message had inspired me. I remember pointing out how much He loves us when we are broken, for in that place we come to understand that He is the one that can give us strength when we're weak.

As the reminder of how God loves me faded, I heard a loud voice call out my name. It startled me back to reality. I stood from leaning against the counter, wiped my face, and cleared my throat to answer my husband's call. From upstairs, he asked if I was ok. I told him, "Yes. Give me a few, I'll be up."

The next words I heard were, "I love you."

I then broke into tears of joy as I had a moment of feeling so grateful that my husband loved me and cared just as Yahshua (Jesus) Loves us and thinks of us when we are out of His view for too long. I then said in my soft voice, "Thank you, Yahshua (Jesus), for putting the blessing of love in my path as I rendered my life back to You. HalleluYah!!"

Psalm 55:22 SHV. Cast thy burden upon the Elohim, and he shall sustain thee: He shall never suffer the righteous to be moved.

Psalm 34:18 SHV. The Lord is nigh unto them that are of a broken heart; and saveth such as be of a contrite spirit.

Heavenly Father,

I thank you for this reader. We come to you this day asking You to teach us how to rest in You. Show us how to let our hearts not be troubled, Father. I ask that You empower the reader to know that You have sent us a comforter for those times when things get rough. It is vital to the heart that we learn to love ourselves and learn to love You. I pray that the reader stands firm, rooted, and determined to trust You and to commune with You. For You can do exceeding abundantly above all that we ask or think according to the power that works in us. We want to say thank You for what You are doing in our lives and for who you purposely place in our paths for our own good. Let us allow You to be the driver of our thoughts and the lover of our soul. We will be careful to give You the Glory and the Honor that is due unto You. Amen.

Lesson 7
Under His Umbrella

Dear Husband,

Allow me to utilize this space to say thank you for delicately picking up my shattered pieces. Just as I was about to give up on love, you came rushing in. Through laughter, patience, peace, and your actions, you show me the true meaning of love. They all are examples of how Yahshua said you are to love your wife as He loves the church. You leave me nothing to worry about, which allows me to close my eyes effortlessly at night. Thank you for being the air that I breathe.

Was it the stride in his walk, the freshly cut beard, the scent of his cologne, or the three-piece suit that grabbed my attention? Maybe it was the laughter that he brought into my life? Whatever it was, I was surely fighting my feelings. There was no way a man could be nice without a motive. They either just wanted sex, or they had the intent to reel you in and then hurt you. I wasn't buying it, but I was certainly looking.

I spent most of my teenage years with one foot in the church and one foot in the world. When I was in church regularly,

I didn't have a true understanding of relationship with Father Yah at all. When I finally decided to go back to church and walk the straight path with Yahshua (Jesus) after the ending of my first marriage, I felt like something was different. It wasn't just that I was broken, it was also the fact that I didn't run back alone. This time I had a four year old to protect and to provide structure for. I *had* to get my life together.

I was never a big dreamer; I didn't have my future planned out like others. But what I learned after taking care of my brothers at a young age was that I never wanted the feeling of bringing a child into the world just to say that I was a mother. My thoughts were that if I was to bring a child into this world, the father and I were going to be a family and we were going do it together. We both had to want to have a family together, so anything different wasn't an option. I had high hopes for me and my first husband. I would never have thought that things were going to end the way that they did. Sadly, I was now left alone to find a clear vision for myself and my son.

Much Needed Surgery

Father Yah had to perform a very intense spiritual surgery on me. He needed someone who had the fruits of the Spirit already produced in them to help nurse a new strength in me. They had to be patient, kind, loving, gentle, faithful, peaceful, good, and full of joy and self-control. And it was obvious that he had the perfect person already lined up for me.

It took a while for my spiritual eyes to adjust to what God was doing. After years of being in a failed marriage, I had lost the idea of what love was supposed to be like. Yah placed married couples around me to provide a healthy reflection of a union. Sadly, I saw it in them but couldn't see it for myself anymore.

When I finally did begin to notice that love was creeping in, I tried hard to keep it at bay.

This man was different, so different that I wasn't sure how to receive or accept everything he did for me. He took me out to elegant dinners, he opened doors for me and introduced me to places I had never even known existed in Rochester. But most importantly, the thing that stood out to me was how attentive and caring he was to my son. Even though I liked how he got along with my child, it took some time for me to let my guard down because of my overprotectiveness toward my son. I was thrilled to see him interact with my boy because, in my mind, anyone that got with me would have to be accepting of my son. He was. That still didn't stop me from being suspicious of him. I couldn't put my finger on why he was being so polite, but his character and approach were out of the norm and I wasn't used to that.

A year went by and there had been nothing but good vibes going on in my life. I was twenty-eight years old and at this point, my son was five. Life had changed for us in such a short period of time. My relationship with the new guy moved like a steady stream and was as deep as the ocean. Before I knew it, I was preparing to be remarried. Essentially, I was experiencing a man who wasn't afraid to show that he loved Father Yah and would eventually play a major part in helping me become closer to our Heavenly Father.

The Second Time Around

Whoever told you that you had to love somebody to get married? I was still learning how to trust for a second time, therefore, when we got married, part of me was invested, and another part of me was coming from the traumatic side. Part of me wanted to tap into revenge and make the ex-husband feel the same pain that I'd experienced while dealing with him. I hadn't yet gotten to the part where love was present with me yet.

I knew it wouldn't be long before the streets would be talking and letting my first husband know that I was remarried. Deep down inside, I knew he would be pissed, and it felt so empowering to have those thoughts. Yes, I knew we shouldn't treat people the way they treated us, but it felt good to know that I would give him the same hurtful energy I'd endured from for so long. I didn't think I deserved the deception that he'd given to me and I wanted him to experience it for himself.

When it came time to get remarried, I didn't fully understand how to confess true love. However, I was willing to learn and allow life on the right path to have its way with me. I was still a work in progress and yet he was patient with the impatience that I carried. Slowly, I had begun to understand that some of the unhealthy things I was bringing into this new marriage had to be addressed.

It was like I'd had an out-of-body experience or something. He'd never said anything to me about my issues, all of a sudden, I just felt like a change needed to happen. I think it was my own convictions letting me see that I had a problem with yelling and arguing during conversations that didn't have a cause for that kind of behavior. It was so bad, that I would walk away from dialogue that needed to be had if I got frustrated. When we were on the phone, I would rudely hang up. One day, I was reminded of the old cliché "it takes two to argue." At that moment, I finally saw myself arguing alone. I had no choice but to calm down. I was starting to truly see myself and understand that I was not in the same environment I'd been in before.

When I think about our first five years of marriage, I realize that it felt like I was in therapy with the best therapist ever. My husband. We needed to learn how to be friends first.

Then we needed to talk about any and everything that needed to be discussed that would allow both of us to understand one another better.

My husband didn't have any biological children at the time. He was careful to assure me that he would never be a father who participated in producing kids and walking out of their lives. He made that very clear to me from the beginning. Yet, I was blessed with the privilege of carefully watching him embrace my son as his own flesh and blood. His actions truly showed me how much he cared. I finally felt it was safe to move forward and grow our family as quickly as we did.

We went from taking care of one son to me conceiving two more sons within the next two years. When he would come home from a hard day at work and find time to play catch with the kids or wrestle around with them and show them love and affection, it brought great joy to them and me. There was more laughter than tears in our household, something I had once been completely unaccustomed to.

Our childhood similarities allowed us some leverage on how to care for our children. After he shared some of his childhood stories with me, we came to realize that we'd both had to look after our siblings at a young age. However, there was one thing he'd been blessed with that I could not relate to because, sadly, I never got to experience it. My husband grew up in a big family, one where they took care of one another just as a family should.

It was unfortunate that when we first met, his mother was on her death bed, may Yah rest her soul. He had Grandma by his side, though, and she was very welcoming from the first time I laid eyes on her. I was grateful for Grandma for she played a great role in my husband's life. She taught him to be independent, responsible and nurturing, all qualities that made our marriage smooth and our life complete.

Family Order

Even though I took good care of my brothers, there was still a frightening feeling of being a new mother and fearing the unknown. I remember when I would say that being a parent didn't come with a manual on how to live. But that was from a place of lacking a true understanding of Yah's Word and of not knowing that He has given us clear instructions on what to do and how we should do it. His rule book is effective and has order. Through Yah, our Heavenly Father, who has already gracefully laid out in His Word that there is an order we should prioritize when it comes to family, I was able to relax and be the best mother I could be.

I'm reminded of an image I saw on the internet of four umbrellas. Under each one, there was listed a biblical family order. The first umbrella showed that we ought to love and acknowledge the Most-High Yah. The second umbrella showed his son Yahshua (Jesus), who was the ultimate sacrifice for you and me. The third showed that under Yahshua (Jesus), the husband would protect, provide, and cover his wife. And the fourth umbrella showed that the wife would comfort, nurture, and teach her children as they learned to obey and love their parents. From those umbrellas and through Yah, I learned that when things were done under the submission and reverence of Yahshua (Jesus), then the biblical and spiritual balance would be clearly shown. Doing things in this order brings so much peace and gratitude to life.

The lesson that I have learned at this part of my life is that Father Yah has made it clear that He knew me in my mother's womb, and He knew the plans He had for me, plans to prosper, and not harm me while giving me a hopeful future. No matter how long it took, He carried me through. He has a purpose for His children.

The Arrival
You Have Arrived at Your Destination!

In the book of Ezekiel, chapter 37:1-14, the Most-High told the prophet Ezekiel to speak to the dry bones and they would come together and live. He then told Ezekiel to speak to the four winds and the slain bodies would have breath in them.

Thank you, Ezekiel, because my dry bones are living now. I was spiritually dead, but I have come alive through the Spirit of the Rauch (Holy Spirit). I'm so grateful that I was able to share with you the many encounters I endured in my past. I now have a clear understanding that my pain wasn't done with the intent to hurt me or to make me suffer. The Most-High needed me so He could redeem and qualify me to be intentionally used by Him.

Each piece of my story entails the strength I never knew I had, but the Father knew that strength was in me all along. Now that my eyes are wide open and I can see how the world has a way of making you feel less than or not enough to fit into certain spaces, He has shown me that I am overqualified by Him. I am here to remind you that you are a chosen people, a generation called out by Father Yah.

We must know that everything is built around time. When the time is right for whatever Yah has planned for you, there is a peaceful feeling that overtakes you and assures you that it's right. I have been prophesied to many times and told that there was a book inside of me. I never acted on it because I never saw the full potential inside of me that others so easily saw. But Father Yah knew, and He knew the hour was not then. I did not yet have a steady foundation under me to help anybody.

Follow me as I share the clarity of knowing now is the time.

In 2019, during what would be the four hundred-year bondage prophecy in the bible, I began to be set free from spiritual bondage. My comprehension of the bible had opened enormously. As I started to walk in the truth of Yah's Word, I began to understand who I was and how I could read the Word of Yah and feel a connection to the Scriptures. The more I read, the more empowered I felt and I grew hungry for more as the days progressed. My collection of books, notes, and technology had increased rapidly, and it was all working together to satiate my hunger and thirst.

I quickly realized that I was attracted to books that entailed information about the history of our ancestors as slaves. It intrigued me to see how all the Information I was coming into was reverting right back to the Word of Yah. Before I knew it, I was taking trips to Barnes and Noble to purchase more books, something I had never taken the time to do before. There was one trip to Barnes and Noble where I picked up a specific book that stood out to me. The title of it was "Slaves in the Family" written by Edward Ball. There I was in the beginning of a newfound love for reading and this book, sitting on a shelf right in front of me, was staring me in the face. Just like all the other things of intent, I believe it was the Most-High's intent for me to lock eyes on that specific book.

I bought it, but I didn't read it right away, it would be about two days later before I finally picked it up. When I did, I found myself drowning in the information that was in that book. I got to this one part that allowed me to hear the voice of Yah through the pages of the book. I read a line that stated, "The Ball family has more than ten thousand pages of information housed in four libraries." The information the author was referring to was all the names of the slaves the Ball family had owned.

The library was a place I rarely visited. It was frustrating to think that for so many years I had never taken advantage of all the information before my eyes, information that lay in those books. Part of me wanted to beat myself up for allowing the enemy to steal valuable learning time from me, but the Spirit of Yah would not let me. He had set a flame of fire burning inside of me that made me want to share certain pieces of what I now know as His Truth. It is His Truth because it is in His Word and He, Himself, has revealed the lines of the words to me through the Rauch (Holy Spirit). My prayer is that after I plant the seed, the Most-High will come along and water it and you will then allow the Rauch (Holy Spirit) to have his way with you like He did with me.

Sometimes people say that the past is the past and to let it be, but I beg to differ. Just as you walked down the path of my life throughout this book and visited areas with me that I thought I was healed from, my past can be used to help or heal someone else. In this instance, I understand that leaving the past in the past would have been the wrong thing to do.

For the longest time, I didn't even understand that the things I had gone through were traumatic. However, going back into my life's history helped me to see the trauma I'd carried all those years and the fact that the trauma had never been dealt with. It's the same way with the Word of Yah. You must go back to the beginning to identify the trauma that has been carried into your today. There is not only healing for you in that process, but also proof, prophecy, and understanding as to why the world we live in today has conveyed so much wickedness in the hearts of the people.

People tend to have wisdom but keep it to themselves. I don't have a full understanding as to why some are that way, but I feel as though it's my due diligence to share my wisdom with you. There is a saying that goes *each one teach one*, that is what I have been known to do. As I share the outlined scriptures with you, it is important that you know they are for your educational understanding and for the purpose of guiding your steps closer to your relationship with the Heavenly Father.

The Torah Teachings

Allow me to share these helpful things with you, things that are important to understand before trying to dive into scripture with the intent of gaining a full understanding. First, make sure you are in a quiet space away from the noise of the world so that things can become intimate between you and the Father. Second, you must pray. But before you pray, examine your heart to ensure it is pure. While you're praying, be sure to ask for eyes to see His Word clearly and ears to hear what the Word is saying to you. Last, be prepared for what you have asked Him for. Often, we pray and ask Yah for things and He blesses us with those things only for us to discover that we're not ready for the blessings like we thought we were.

The first five books in the bible are The Law of Moses. The Hebrew name for them is the Torah. The Hebrew word for Torah is "law."

Here is a summary to help you when you go to read these books:

1. Genesis:

Genesis means *in the beginning*. It deals with Creation, Adam and Eve, the flood, the patriarchs and the matriarchs of the Hebrew people, and it ends with the descent of Jacob and his family into Egypt. It also contains the commandment of circumcision and God's promise to Abraham that he would receive the Land of Israel and that his descendants would be a major, positive influence on the entire world.

2. Exodus:

Although in Greek Exodus means *going out,* which explains the actual Hebrew exodus from Egypt, in Yah's original language of Hebrew, Exodus means *names*, which refers to the names of the Hebrews who entered Egypt with Jacob. This second book of the Torah deals with their exile, their enslavement, their suffering, the life of Moses, his initial prophecies, the ten plagues, and the exodus. It also describes the revelation at Mt. Sinai where the Hebrew people received the Ten Commandments and the Written and Oral Torah.

3. Leviticus:

Leviticus means *He called*. In this book, The Most-High calls to Moses and informs him in detail of the laws regarding the festivals, priests, and the temple service. The Hebrew code of morality, ethics, and charity also appear in Leviticus, including the famous commandment to *love your neighbor as yourself* (Leviticus 19:18).

4. Numbers:

Numbers means *in the desert* and it details the travels, battles, and struggles of the Hebrews during their forty year sojourn in the desert after the exodus. It records a census of the tribes, the positioning of each tribe when they camped and traveled, their rebellion, and the events surrounding the sending of spies into Israel. Numbers ends with the capture of the east bank of the Jordan River and the subsequent settlement there of the tribes of Reuben and Gad.

5. Deuteronomy:

Deuteronomy means *words*, which refers to Moses' address to the Hebrew people before his death. This prophetic farewell includes rebuke, encouragement, warnings, and prophecies. In it, there are commandments that would only apply in the land of Israel and that govern interaction with other nations. New commandments are given, many of which concern the courts and justice system. After his farewell, Moses wrote thirteen complete copies of the Torah, gave one to each tribe, and placed one in Holy Ark. The five books close with the death of the greatest of all prophets and the humblest of all men, Moses.

The elements that show through the contents of those five books are the history of Israel, the Kingdom of Yah, and the law.

A Lesson from History

Have you ever decided to search for a deeper understanding of slavery and its history? Well, it is through those five main books that I searched and now understand my history even more. I also understand the lineage from which I have come. I am a remnant of the children of Israel and I have been called out, chosen for this very moment, to help direct you back to the Word of Yah so that He can reveal to you what is solely for you.

It is in the Word of Yah that He expresses His great love for His children, but also His anger because of their disobedience. He makes it real concise that they were scattered amongst the earth for a while, but He will come back for them. He promised to gather them from all four corners of the earth and bring them back to their land. Yes, this is a book of the past, but it is filled with a prophecy that has yet to be fulfilled.

It is with great intent that I encourage you to read, with an understanding, of your spiritual history. It is with a changed heart that I express my gratitude to Yahshua (Jesus) for advocating for me daily each time that I wake up and mess up. I know that it is not by our works or anything that we have done special, but that He has chosen us because He loves us and He cares for us. He has separated us for a special purpose only He knows. Going back to the past of my own life and digging through it to understand Father Yah and Yahshua (Jesus) even more has increased my relationship with Him and has allowed me to be in tune with His Word and to look toward His Kingdom.

I am speaking to your atmosphere as you read this. "You shall live and not die. You shall awaken and rise to the occasion, to the assignment of whatever He has for you. My assignment was to write this book so that you are given directions and so that you may know that it is ok to disrupt the traditions of man, to disrupt their protocol, and to dig a little deeper and stretch a little wider, all under the authority of Yah so that you can be free indeed.

www.ingramcontent.com/pod-product-compliance
Lightning Source LLC
Chambersburg PA
CBHW030225170426
43194CB00007BA/862